POLITICS AND THE
ENGLISH LANGUAGE

POLITICS AND THE ENGLISH LANGUAGE

by

George Orwell
1946

Most people who bother with the matter at all would admit that the English language is in a bad way, but it is generally assumed that we cannot by conscious action do anything about it. Our civilization is decadent and our language — so the argument runs — must inevitably share in the general collapse. It follows that any struggle against the abuse of language is a sentimental archaism, like preferring candles to electric light or hansom cabs to aeroplanes. Underneath this lies the half-conscious belief that language is a natural growth and not an instrument which we shape for our own purposes.

Now, it is clear that the decline of a language must ultimately have political and economic causes: it is not due simply to the bad influence of this or that individual writer. But an effect can become a cause, reinforcing the original cause and producing the same effect in an intensified form, and so on indefinitely. A man may take to drink because he feels himself to be a failure, and then fail all the more completely because he drinks. It is rather the same thing that is happening to the English language. It becomes ugly and inaccurate because our thoughts are foolish, but the slovenliness of our language makes it easier for us to have foolish thoughts. The point is that the process is reversible. Modern English, especially written English, is full of bad habits which spread by imitation and which can be avoided if one is willing to take the necessary trouble. If one gets rid of these habits one can think more clearly, and to think clearly is a necessary first step toward political regeneration: so that the fight against bad English is not frivolous and is not the exclusive concern of professional writers. I will come back to this presently, and I hope that by that time the meaning of what I have said here will have become clearer.

Meanwhile, here are five specimens of the English language as it is now habitually written.

These five passages have not been picked out because they are especially bad — I could have quoted far worse if I had chosen — but because they illustrate various of the mental vices from which we now suffer. They are a little below the average, but are fairly representative examples. I number them so that I can refer back to them when necessary:

I am not, indeed, sure whether it is not true to say that the Milton who once seemed not unlike a seventeenth-century Shelley had not become, out of an experience ever more bitter in each year, more alien [sic] to the founder of that Jesuit sect which nothing could induce him to tolerate.

-Professor Harold Laski

(Essay in Freedom of Expression)

Above all, we cannot play ducks and drakes with a native battery of idioms which prescribes egregious collocations of vocables as the Basic put up with for tolerate , or put at a loss for bewilder .

-Professor Lancelot Hogben (Interglossia)

On the one side we have the free personality: by definition it is not neurotic, for it has neither conflict nor dream. Its desires, such as they are, are transparent, for they are just what institutional approval keeps in the forefront of consciousness; another institutional pattern would alter their number and intensity; there is little in them that is natural, irreducible, or culturally dangerous. But on the other side , the social bond itself is nothing but the mutual reflection of these self-secure integrities.

Recall the definition of love. Is not this the very picture of a small academic? Where is there a place in this hall of mirrors for either personality or fraternity?

-Essay on psychology in Politics (New York)

All the "best people" from the gentlemen's clubs, and all the frantic fascist captains, united in common hatred of Socialism and bestial horror at the rising tide of the mass revolutionary movement, have turned to acts of provocation, to foul incendiarism, to medieval legends of poisoned wells, to legalize their own destruction of proletarian organizations, and rouse the agitated petty-bourgeoise to chauvinistic fervor on behalf of the fight against the revolutionary way out of the crisis.

-Communist pamphlet

If a new spirit is to be infused into this old country, there is one thorny and contentious reform which must be tackled, and that is the humanization and galvanization of the B.B.C. Timidity here will bespeak canker and atrophy of the soul. The heart of Britain may be sound and of strong beat, for instance, but the British lion's roar at present is like that of Bottom in Shakespeare's A Midsummer Night's Dream — as gentle as any sucking dove. A virile new

Britain cannot continue indefinitely to be traduced in the eyes or rather ears, of the world by the effete languors of Langham Place, brazenly masquerading as "standard English." When the Voice of Britain is heard at nine

o'clock, better far and infinitely less ludicrous to hear aitches honestly dropped than the present priggish, inflated, inhibited, school-ma ' amish arch braying of blameless bashful mewing maidens!

-Letter in Tribune

Each of these passages has faults of its own, but, quite apart from avoidable ugliness, two qualities are common to all of them. The first is staleness of imagery; the other is lack of precision. The writer either has a meaning and cannot express it, or he inadvertently says something else, or he is almost indifferent as to whether his words mean anything or not. This mixture of vagueness and sheer incompetence is the most marked characteristic of modern

English prose, and especially of any kind of political writing. As soon as certain topics are raised, the concrete melts into the abstract and no one seems able to think of turns of speech that are not hackneyed: prose consists less and

less of words chosen for the sake of their meaning, and more and more of phrases tacked together like the sections of a prefabricated henhouse. I list below, with notes and examples, various of the tricks by means of which the work of prose construction is habitually dodged:

Dying metaphors. A newly invented metaphor assists thought by evoking a visual image, while on the other hand a metaphor which is technically "dead" (e.g. iron resolution) has in effect reverted to being an ordinary word and can generally be used without loss of vividness. But in between these two classes there is a huge dump of worn-out metaphors which have lost all evocative power and are merely used because they save people the trouble of inventing phrases for themselves. Examples are: Ring the changes on, take up the cudgel for, toe the line, ride roughshod over, stand shoulder to shoulder with, play into the hands of, no axe to grind, grist to the mill, fishing in troubled waters, on the order of the day, Achilles' heel, swan song, hotbed . Many of these are used without knowledge of their meaning (what is a "rift," for instance?), and incompatible metaphors are frequently mixed, a sure sign that the writer is not interested in what he is saying. Some metaphors now current have been twisted out of their original meaning withouth those who use them even being aware of the fact. For example, toe the line is sometimes written as tow the line . Another example is the hammer and the anvil , now always used with the implication that the anvil gets the worst of it. In real life it is always the anvil that breaks the hammer, never the other way about: a writer who stopped to think what he was saying would avoid perverting the original phrase.

Operators or verbal false limbs. These save the trouble of picking out appropriate verbs and nouns, and at the same time pad each sentence with extra syllables which give it an appearance of symmetry. Characteristic phrases are render inoperative, militate against, make contact with, be subjected to, give rise to, give grounds for, have the effect of, play a leading part (role) in, make itself felt, take effect, exhibit a tendency to, serve the purpose of, etc., etc . The keynote is the elimination of simple verbs. Instead of being a single word, such as break, stop, spoil, mend, kill , a verb becomes a phrase , made up of a noun or adjective tacked on to some general-purpose verb such as prove, serve, form, play, render . In addition, the passive voice is wherever possible used in preference to the active, and noun constructions are used instead of gerunds (by examination of instead of by examining) . The range of verbs is further cut down by means of the -ize and de- formations, and the banal statements are given an appearance of profundity by means of the not un- formation. Simple conjunctions and prepositions are replaced by such phrases as with respect to, having regard to, the fact that, by dint of, in view of, in the

interests of, on the hypothesis that ; and the ends of sentences are saved by anticlimax by such resounding commonplaces as greatly to be desired, cannot be left out of account, a development to be expected in the near future, deserving of serious consideration, brought to a satisfactory conclusion , and so on and so forth.

Pretentious diction. Words like phenomenon, element, individual (as noun), objective, categorical, effective, virtual, basic, primary, promote, constitute, exhibit, exploit, utilize, eliminate, liquidate , are used to dress up a simple statement and give an aire of scientific impartiality to biased judgements.

Adjectives like epoch-making, epic, historic, unforgettable, triumphant, age-old, inevitable, inexorable, veritable , are used to dignify the sordid process of international politics, while writing that aims at glorifying war usually takes on an archaic color, its characteristic words being: realm, throne, chariot, mailed fist, trident, sword, shield, buckler, banner, jackboot,clarion . Foreign words and expressions such as cul de sac, ancien r&eacutgime, deus ex machine, mutatis mutandis, status quo, gleichschaltung, Weltanschauung , are used to give an air of culture and elegance. Except for the usefulabbreviations i.e., e.g. , and etc. , there is no real need for any of the hundreds of foreign phrases now current in the English language. Bad writers, and especially scientific, political, and sociological writers, are nearly always haunted by the notion that Latin or Greek words are grander than Saxon ones, and unnecessary words like expedite, ameliorate, predict, extraneous, deracinated, clandestine, subaqueous , and hundreds of others constantly gain ground from their Anglo-Saxon numbers. The jargon peculiar to Marxist writing (hyena, hangman, cannibal, petty bourgeois, these gentry, lackey, flunkey, mad dog. White Guard , etc.) consists largely of words translated from Russian, German, or French; but the normal way of coining a new word is to use Latin or Greek root with the appropriate affix and, where necessary, the size formation. It is often easier to make up words of this kind (deregionalize, impermissible, extramarital, non-f ragmentary and so forth) than to think up the English words that will cover one's meaning. The result, in general, is an increase in slovenliness and vagueness.

Meaningless words. In certain kinds of writing, particularly in art criticism and literary criticism, it is normal to come across long passages which are almost completely lacking in meaning. Words like romantic, plastic, values, human, dead, sentimental, natural, vitality , as used in art criticism, are strictly meaningless, in the sense that they not only do not point to any discoverable object, but are hardly ever expected to do so by the reader. When one critic writes, "The outstanding feature of Mr. X's work is its living quality," while another writes, "The immediately striking thing about Mr. X's work is its peculiar deadness, " the reader accepts this as a simple difference opinion. If words like black and white were involved, instead of the jargon

words dead and living, he would see at once that language was being used in an improper way. Many political words are similarly abused. The word Fascism has now no meaning except in so far as it signifies "something not desirable." The

words democracy, socialism, freedom, patriotic, realistic, justice have each of them several different meanings which cannot be reconciled with one another. In the case of a word like democracy, not only is there no agreed definition, but

the attempt to make one is resisted from all sides. It is almost universally felt that when we call a country democratic we are praising it: consequently the defenders of every kind of regime claim that it is a democracy, and fear that they might have to stop using that word if it were tied down to any one meaning.

Words of this kind are often used in a consciously dishonest way. That is, the person who uses them has his own private definition, but allows his hearer to think he means something quite different. Statements like Marshal Retain was a true patriot. The Soviet press is the freest in the world. The Catholic Church is opposed to persecution, are almost always made with intent to deceive. Other words used in variable meanings, in most cases more or less dishonestly, are: class, totalitarian, science, progressive, reactionary, bourgeois, equality.

Now that I have made this catalogue of swindles and perversions, let me give another example of the kind of writing that they lead to. This time it must of its nature be an imaginary one. I am going to translate a passage of good

English into modern English of the worst sort. Here is a well-known verse from Ecclesiastes :

I returned and saw under the sun, that the race is not to the swift, nor the battle to the strong, neither yet bread to the wise, nor yet riches to men of understanding, nor yet favour to men of skill; but time and chance happeneth to them all.

Here it is in modern English:

Objective considerations of contemporary phenomena compel the conclusion that success or failure in competitive activities exhibits no tendency to be commensurate with innate capacity, but that a considerable element of the

unpredictable must invariably be taken into account.

This is a parody, but not a very gross one. Exhibit (3) above, for instance, contains several patches of the same kind of English. It will be seen that I have not made a full translation. The beginning and ending of the sentence follow the original meaning fairly closely, but in the middle the concrete illustrations — race, battle, bread — dissolve into the vague phrases "success or failure in competitive activities." This had to be so, because no modern writer of the kind I am discussing — no one capable of using phrases like "objective considerations of contemporary phenomena" — would ever tabulate his thoughts in that precise and detailed way. The whole tendency of modern prose is away from concreteness. Now analyze these two sentences a little more closely.

The first contains forty-nine words but only sixty syllables, and all its words are those of everyday life. The second contains thirty-eight words of ninety syllables: eighteen of those words are from Latin roots, and one from Greek. The first sentence contains six vivid images, and only one phrase ("time and chance") that could be called vague. The second contains not a single fresh, arresting phrase, and in spite of its ninety syllables it gives only a shortened version of the meaning contained in the first. Yet without a doubt it is the second kind of sentence that is gaining ground in modern English. I do not want to exaggerate. This kind of writing is not yet universal, and outcrops of simplicity will occur here and there in the worst-written page. Still, if you or I were told to write a few lines on the uncertainty of human fortunes, we should probably come much nearer to my imaginary sentence than to the one from Ecclesiastes. As I have tried to show, modern writing at its worst does not consist in picking out words for the sake of their meaning and inventing images in order to make the meaning clearer. It consists in gumming together long strips of words which have already been set in order by someone else, and making the results presentable by sheer humbug. The attraction of this way of writing is that it is easy. It is easier — even quicker, once you have the habit — to say In my opinion it is not an unjustifiable assumption that than to say I think. If you use ready-made phrases, you not only don't have to hunt about for the words; you also don't have to bother with the rhythms of your sentences since these phrases are generally so arranged as to be more or less euphonious.

When you are composing in a hurry — when you are dictating to a stenographer, for instance, or making a public speech — it is natural to fall into a pretentious. Latinized style. Tags like a consideration which we should do well

to bear in mind or a conclusion to which all of us would readily assent will save many a sentence from coming down with a bump. By using stale metaphors, similes, and idioms, you save much mental effort, at the cost of leaving your meaning vague, not only for your reader but for yourself. This is the significance of mixed metaphors. The sole aim of a metaphor is to call up a visual image. When these images clash — as in The Fascist octopus has sung its swan song, the jackboot is thrown into the melting pot — it can be taken as certain that the writer is not seeing a mental image of the objects he is naming; in other words he is not really thinking. Look again at the examples I gave at the beginning of this essay. Professor Laski (1) uses five negatives in fifty three words. One of these is superfluous, making nonsense of the whole passage, and in addition there is the slip — alien for akin — making further nonsense, and several avoidable pieces of clumsiness which increase the general vagueness. Professor Hogben (2) plays ducks and drakes with a battery which is able to write prescriptions, and, while disapproving of the everyday phrase put up with, is unwilling to look egregious up in the dictionary and see what it means; (3), if one takes an uncharitable attitude towards it, is simply meaningless: probably one could work out its intended meaning by reading the whole of the article in which it occurs. In (4), the writer knows more or less what he wants to say, but anaccumulation of stale phrases chokes him like tea leaves blocking a sink. In (5), words and meaning have almost parted company.

People who write in this manner usually have a general emotional meaning — they dislike one thing and want to express solidarity with another — but they are not interested in the detail of what they are saying. A scrupulous writer, in

every sentence that he writes, will ask himself at least four questions, thus:

What am I trying to say?

What words will express it?

What image or idiom will make it clearer?

Is this image fresh enough to have an effect? And he will probably ask himself two more: Could I put it more shortly?

Have I said anything that is avoidably ugly?

But you are not obliged to go to all this trouble. You can shirk it by simply throwing your mind open and letting the ready-made phrases come crowding in. The will construct your sentences for you — even think your thoughts for you, to a certain extent — and at need they will perform the important service of partially concealing your meaning even from yourself. It is at this point that the special connection between politics and the debasement of language becomes

clear .

In our time it is broadly true that political writing is bad writing. Where it is not true, it will generally be found that the writer is some kind of rebel, expressing his private opinions and not a "party line." Orthodoxy, of whatever color, seems to demand a lifeless, imitative style. The political dialects to be found in pamphlets, leading articles, manifestoes. White papers and the speeches of undersecretaries do, of course, vary from party to party, but they are all alike in that one almost never finds in them a fresh, vivid, homemade turn of speech. When one watches some tired hack on the platform mechanically repeating the familiar phrases — bestial, atrocities, iron heel, bloodstained tyranny, free peoples of the world, stand shoulder to shoulder — one often has a curious feeling that one is not watching a live human being but some kind of dummy: a feeling which suddenly becomes stronger at moments when the light catches the speaker's spectacles and turns them into blank discs which seem to have no eyes behind them. And this is not altogether fanciful. A speaker who uses that kind of phraseology has gone some distance toward turning himself into a machine. The appropriate noises are coming out of his larynx, but his brain is not involved as it would be if he were choosing his words for himself. If the speech he is making is one that he isaccustomed to make over and over again, he may be almost unconscious of what he is saying, as one is when one utters the responses in church. And this reduced state of consciousness, if not indispensable, is at any rate favorable to political conformity.

In our time, political speech and writing are largely the defense of the indefensible. Things like the continuance of British rule in India, the Russian purges and deportations, the dropping of the atom bombs on Japan, can indeed be defended, but only by arguments which are too brutal for most people to face, and which do not square with the professed aims of the political parties. Thus political language has to consist largely of euphemism., question-begging and sheer cloudy vagueness. Defenseless villages are bombarded from the air, the inhabitants driven out into the countryside, the cattle machine-gunned, the huts

set on fire with incendiary bullets: this is called pacification. Millions of peasants are robbed of their farms and sent trudging along the roads with no more than they can carry: this is called transfer of population or rectification of frontiers. People are imprisoned for years without trial, or shot in the back of the neck or sent to die of scurvy in Arctic lumber camps: this is called elimination of unreliable elements. Such phraseology is needed if one wants to name things without calling up mental pictures of them. Consider for instance some comfortable English professor defending Russian totalitarianism. He cannot say outright, "I believe in killing off your opponents when you can get good results by doing so." Probably, therefore, he will say something like this:

While freely conceding that the Soviet regime exhibits certain features which the humanitarian may be inclined to deplore, we must, I think, agree that a certain curtailment of the right to political opposition is an unavoidable concomitant of transitional periods, and that the rigors which the Russian people have been called upon to undergo have been amply justified in the sphere of concrete achievement.

The inflated style itself is a kind of euphemism. A mass of Latin words falls upon the facts like soft snow, blurring the outline and covering up all the details. The great enemy of clear language is insincerity. When there is a gap between one's real and one's declared aims, one turns as it were instinctively to long words and exhausted idioms, like a cuttlefish spurting out ink. In our age there is no such thing as "keeping out of politics." All issues are political issues, and politics itself is a mass of lies, evasions, folly, hatred, and schizophrenia. When the general atmosphere is bad, language must suffer. I should expect to find — this is a guess which I have not sufficient knowledge to verify — that the German, Russian and Italian languages have all deteriorated in the last ten or fifteen years, as a result of dictatorship.

But if thought corrupts language, language can also corrupt thought. A bad usage can spread by tradition and imitation even among people who should and do know better. The debased language that I have been discussing is in some ways very convenient. Phrases like a not unjustifiable assumption, leaves much to be desired, would serve no good purpose, a consideration which we should do well to bear in mind, are a continuous temptation, a packet of aspirins always at one's elbow. Look back through this essay, and for certain you will find that I have again and again committed the very faults I am protesting against. By this morning's post I have received a pamphlet dealing with conditions in Germany.

The author tells me that he "felt impelled" to write it. I open it at random, and here is almost the first sentence I see: "[The Allies] have an opportunity not only of achieving a radical transformation of Germany's social and political structure in such a way as to avoid a nationalistic reaction in Germany itself, but at the same time of laying the foundations of a co-operative and unified Europe." You see, he "feels impelled" to write — feels, presumably, that he has

something new to say — and yet his words, like cavalry horses answering the bugle, group themselves automatically into the familiar dreary pattern. This invasion of one's mind by ready-made phrases (lay the foundations, achieve a

radical transformation) can only be prevented if one is constantly on guard against them, and every such phrase anaesthetizes a portion of one's brain.

I said earlier that the decadence of our language is probably curable. Those who deny this would argue, if they produced an argument at all, that language merely reflects existing social conditions, and that we cannot influence its

development by any direct tinkering with words and

constructions. So far as the general tone or spirit of a language goes, this may be true, but it is not true in detail.

Silly words and expressions have often disappeared, not through any evolutionary process but owing to the conscious action of a minority. Two recent examples were explore every avenue and leave no stone unturned , which were

killed by the jeers of a few journalists. There is a long list of flyblown metaphors which could similarly be got rid of if enough people would interest themselves in the job; and it should also be possible to laugh the not un formation out of existence, to reduce the amount of Latin and Greek in the

average sentence, to drive out foreign phrases and strayed scientific words, and, in general, to make pretentiousness unfashionable. But all these are minor points. The defense of the English language implies more than this, and perhaps it is best to start by saying what it does not imply.

To begin with it has nothing to do with archaism, with the salvaging of obsolete words and turns of speech, or with the setting up of a "standard English" which must never be departed from. On the contrary, it is especially concerned with the scrapping of every word or idiom which has outworn its usefulness. It has nothing to do with correct grammar and syntax, which are of no importance so long as one makes one's meaning clear, or with the avoidance of Americanisms, or with having what is called a "good prose style." On the other hand, it is not concerned with fake simplicity and the attempt to make written English

colloquial. Nor does it even imply in every case preferring the Saxon word to the Latin one, though it does imply using the fewest and shortest words that will cover one's meaning. What is above all needed is to let the meaning choose the word, and not the other way around. In prose, the worst thing one can do with words is surrender to them. When yo think of a concrete object, you think wordlessly, and then, if you want to describe the thing you have been visualizing you probably hunt about until you find the exact words that seem to fit it. When you think of something abstract you are more inclined to use words from the start, and unless you make a conscious effort to prevent it, the existing dialect will come rushing in and do the job for you, at the expense of blurring or even changing your meaning. Probably it is better to put off using words as long as possible and get one's meaning as clear as one can through pictures and sensations. Afterward one can choose — not simply accept — the phrases that will best cover the meaning, and then switch round and decide what impressions one's words are likely to mak on another person. This last effort of the mind cuts out all stale or mixed images, all prefabricated phrases, needless repetitions, and humbug and vagueness generally. But one can often be in doubt about the effect of a word or a phrase, and one needs rules that one can rely on when instinct fails. I think the following rules will cover most cases:

Never use a metaphor, simile, or other figure of speech which you are used to seeing in print .

Never us a long word where a short one will do. If it is possible to cut a word out, always cut it out. Never use the passive where you can use the active.

Never use a foreign phrase, a scientific word, or a jargon word if you can think of an everyday English equivalent.

Break any of these rules sooner than say anything outright barbarous.

These rules sound elementary, and so they are, but they demand a deep change of attitude in anyone who has grown used to writing in the style now fashionable.

One could keep all of them and still write bad English, but one could not write the kind of stuff that I quoted in those five specimens at the beginning of this article .

I have not here been considering the literary use of language, but merely language as an instrument for expressing and not for concealing or preventing thought. Stuart Chase and others have come near to claiming that all abstract words are meaningless, and have used this as a pretext for advocating a kind of political quietism. Since you don't know what Fascism is, how can you struggle against Fascism? One need not swallow such absurdities as this, but one ought to recognize that the present political chaos is connected with the decay of language, and that one can probably bring about some improvement by starting at the verbal end. If you simplify your English, you are freed from the worst follies of orthodoxy. You cannot speak any of the necessary dialects, and when you make a stupid remark its stupidity will be obvious, even to yourself.

Political language — and with variations this is true of all political parties, from Conservatives to Anarchists — is designed to make lies sound truthful and murder respectable, and to give an appearance of solidity to pure wind. One

cannot change this all in a moment, but one can at least change one's own habits, and from time to time one can even, if one jeers loudly enough, send some worn-out and useless phrase — some jackboot, Achilles' heel, hotbed,

melting pot, acid test, veritable inferno, or other lump of verbal refuse into the dustbin, where it belongs.

GEORGE ORWELL

Eric Arthur Blair (25 June 1903 – 21 January 1950),
[1] better known by his pen name **George Orwell**, was an
English novelist and essayist, journalist and critic.[2] His
work is characterised by lucid prose, biting social criticism,
opposition to totalitarianism, and outspoken support
of democratic socialism.[3][4][5][6]

As a writer, Orwell produced literary criticism and poetry,
fiction and polemical journalism; and is best known for
the allegorical novella *Animal Farm* (1945) and
the dystopian novel *Nineteen Eighty-Four* (1949). His non-
fiction works, including *The Road to Wigan Pier* (1937),
documenting his experience of working-class life in the north
of England, and *Homage to Catalonia* (1938), an account of
his experiences soldiering for the Republican faction of
the Spanish Civil War (1936–1939), are as critically

respected as his essays on politics and literature, language and culture. In 2008, *The Times* ranked George Orwell second among "The 50 greatest British writers since 1945". [7]

Orwell's work remains influential in popular culture and in political culture, and the adjective "Orwellian"—describing totalitarian and authoritarian social practices—is part of the English language, like many of his neologisms, such as "Big Brother", "Thought Police", "Two Minutes Hate", "Room 101", "memory hole", "Newspeak", "doublethink", "proles", "unperson", and "thoughtcrime".[8] [9]

Second World War and *Animal Farm*

A photo of Orwell, c. 1940, digitally coloured

At the outbreak of the Second World War, Orwell's wife Eileen started working in the Censorship Department of the Ministry of Information in central London, staying during he week with her family in Greenwich. Orwell also submitted his name to the Central Register for war work, but nothing transpired. "They won't have me in the army, at any rate at present, because of my lungs", Orwell told Geoffrey Gorer. He returned to Wallington, and in late 1939 he wrote material for his first collection of essays, *Inside the Whale*. For the next year he was occupied writing reviews for plays, films and books for *The Listener*, *Time and Tide* and *New Adelphi*. On 29 March 1940 his long association with *Tribune* began[85] with a review of a sergeant's account of Napoleon's retreat from Moscow. At the beginning of 1940, the first edition of Connolly's *Horizon* appeared, and this provided a new outlet for Orwell's work as well as new literary contacts. In May the Orwells took lease of a flat in London at Dorset Chambers, Chagford Street, Marylebone. It was the time of the Dunkirk evacuation and the death in France of Eileen's brother Lawrence caused her considerable grief and long-term depression. Throughout this period Orwell kept a wartime diary.[86]

Orwell was declared "unfit for any kind of military service" by the Medical Board in June, but soon afterwards found an opportunity to become involved in war activities by joining the Home Guard.[87] He shared Tom Wintringham's socialist vision for the Home Guard as a revolutionary People's Militia. His lecture notes for instructing platoon members include advice on street fighting, field fortifications, and the use of mortars of various kinds. Sergeant Orwell managed to recruit Fredric Warburg to his unit. During the Battle of Britain he used to spend weekends with Warburg and his new Zionist friend, Tosco Fyvel, at Warburg's house at Twyford, Berkshire. At Wallington he worked on

"England Your England" and in London wrote reviews for various periodicals. Visiting Eileen's family in Greenwich brought him face-to-face with the effects of the Blitz on East London. In mid-1940, Warburg, Fyvel and Orwell planned Searchlight Books. Eleven volumes eventually appeared, of which Orwell's *The Lion and the Unicorn: Socialism and the English Genius*, published on 19 February 1941, was the first.[88]

Early in 1941 he began to write for the American *Partisan Review* which linked Orwell with The New York Intellectuals who were also anti-Stalinist,[89] and contributed to the Gollancz anthology *The Betrayal of the Left*, written in the light of the Molotov–Ribbentrop Pact (although Orwell referred to it as the Russo-German Pact and the Hitler-Stalin Pact[90]). He also applied unsuccessfully for a job at the Air Ministry. Meanwhile, he was still writing reviews of books and plays and at this time met the novelist Anthony Powell. He also took part in a few radio broadcasts for the Eastern Service of the BBC. In March the Orwells moved to a seventh-floor flat at Langford Court, St John's Wood, while at Wallington Orwell was "digging for victory" by planting potatoes.

> One could not have a better example of the moral and emotional shallowness of our time, than the fact that we are now all more or less pro Stalin. This disgusting murderer is temporarily on our side, and so the purges, etc., are suddenly forgotten.
>
> — George Orwell, in his war-time diary, 3 July 1941[91]

In August 1941, Orwell finally obtained "war work" when he was taken on full-time by the BBC's Eastern Service. He supervised cultural broadcasts to India to counter propaganda from Nazi Germany designed to undermine Imperial links. This was Orwell's first experience of the rigid conformity of life in an office, and it gave him an opportunity to create cultural programmes with contributions from T. S. Eliot, Dylan Thomas, E. M. Forster, Ahmed Ali, Mulk Raj Anand, and William Empson among others.

At the end of August he had a dinner with H. G. Wells which degenerated into a row because Wells had taken offence at observations Orwell made about him in a *Horizon* article. In October Orwell had a bout of bronchitis and the illness recurred frequently. David Astor was looking for a provocative contributor for *The Observer* and invited Orwell to write for him—the first article appearing in March 1942. In early 1942 Eileen changed jobs to work at the Ministry of Food and in mid-1942 the Orwells moved to a larger flat, a ground floor and basement, 10a Mortimer Crescent in Maida Vale/Kilburn—"the kind of lower-middle-class ambience that Orwell thought was London at its best." Around the same time Orwell's mother and sister Avril, who had found work in a sheet-metal factory behind King's Cross Station, moved into a flat close to George and Eileen.[92]

Orwell spoke on many BBC and other broadcasts, but no recordings are known to survive.[93][94][95]

At the BBC, Orwell introduced *Voice*, a literary programme for his Indian broadcasts, and by now was leading an active social life with literary friends, particularly on the political left. Late in 1942, he started writing regularly for the left-wing weekly *Tribune*[96]:306[97]:441 directed by Labour MPs Aneurin Bevan and George Strauss. In March 1943 Orwell's mother died and around the same time he told Moore he was starting work on a new book, which turned out to be *Animal Farm*.

In September 1943, Orwell resigned from the BBC post that he had occupied for two years.[98]:352 His resignation followed a report confirming his fears that few Indians listened to the broadcasts,[99] but he was also keen to concentrate on writing *Animal Farm*. Just six days before his last day of service, on 24 November 1943, his adaptation of the fairy tale, Hans Christian Andersen's *The Emperor's New Clothes* was broadcast. It was a genre in which he was greatly interested and which appeared on *Animal Farm*'s title-page.[100] At this time he also resigned from the Home Guard on medical grounds.[101]

In November 1943, Orwell was appointed literary editor at *Tribune*, where his assistant was his old friend Jon Kimche. Orwell was on staff until early 1945, writing over 80 book reviews[102] and on 3 December 1943 started his regular personal column, "As I Please", usually addressing three or four subjects in each.[103] He was still writing reviews for other magazines, including *Partisan Review*, *Horizon*, and the New York *Nation* and becoming a respected pundit among left-wing circles but also a close friend of people on the right such as Powell, Astor and Malcolm Muggeridge. By April 1944 *Animal Farm* was ready for publication. Gollancz refused to publish it, considering it an attack on the Soviet regime which was a crucial ally in the war. A similar fate was met from other publishers (including T. S. Eliot at Faber and Faber) until Jonathan Cape agreed to take it.

In May the Orwells had the opportunity to adopt a child, thanks to the contacts of Eileen's sister Gwen O'Shaughnessy, then a doctor in Newcastle upon Tyne. In June a V-1 flying bomb struck Mortimer Crescent and the Orwells had to find somewhere else to live. Orwell had to scrabble around in the rubble for his collection of books, which he had finally managed to transfer from Wallington, carting them away in a wheelbarrow.

Another blow was Cape's reversal of his plan to publish *Animal Farm*. The decision followed his personal visit to Peter Smollett, an official at the Ministry of Information. Smollett was later identified as a Soviet agent. [104][105]

The Orwells spent some time in the North East, near Carlton, County Durham, dealing with matters in the adoption of a boy whom they named Richard Horatio Blair.[106] By September 1944 they had set up home in Islington, at 27b Canonbury Square.[107] Baby Richard joined them there, and Eileen gave up her work at the Ministry of Food to look after her family. Secker & Warburg had agreed to publish *Animal Farm*, planned for the following March, although it did not appear in print until August 1945. By February 1945 David Astor had invited Orwell to become a war correspondent for the *Observer*. Orwell had been looking for the opportunity throughout the war, but his failed medical reports prevented him from being allowed anywhere near action. He went to Paris after the liberation of France and to Cologne once it had been occupied by the Allies.

It was while he was there that Eileen went into hospital for a hysterectomy and died under anaesthetic on 29 March 1945. She had not given Orwell much notice about this operation because of worries about the cost and because she expected to make a speedy recovery. Orwell returned home for a while and then went back to Europe. He returned finally to London to cover the 1945 general election at the beginning of July. *Animal Farm: A Fairy Story* was published in Britain on 17 August 1945, and a year later in the US, on 26 August 1946.

Jura and *Nineteen Eighty-Four*

Animal Farm had particular resonance in the post-war climate and its worldwide success made Orwell a sought-after figure. For the next four years, Orwell mixed journalistic work—mainly for *Tribune*, *The Observer* and the *Manchester Evening News*, though he also contributed to many small-circulation political and literary magazines—

with writing his best-known work, *Nineteen Eighty-Four*, which was published in 1949.

Barnhill on the Isle of Jura, Scotland. Orwell completed *Nineteen Eighty-Four* while living in the farmhouse.

In the year following Eileen's death he published around 130 articles and a selection of his *Critical Essays*, while remaining active in various political lobbying campaigns. He employed a housekeeper, Susan Watson, to look after his adopted son at the Islington flat, which visitors now described as "bleak". In September he spent a fortnight on the island of Jura in the Inner Hebrides and saw it as a place to escape from the hassle of London literary life. David Astor was instrumental in arranging a place for Orwell on Jura. [108] Astor's family owned Scottish estates in the area and a fellow Old Etonian, Robin Fletcher, had a property on the island. In late 1945 and early 1946 Orwell made several hopeless and unwelcome marriage proposals to younger women, including Celia Kirwan (who later became Arthur Koestler's sister-in-law), Ann Popham who happened to live in the same block of flats and Sonia Brownell, one of Connolly's coterie at the *Horizon* office. Orwell suffered a tubercular haemorrhage in February 1946 but disguised his illness. In 1945 or early 1946, while still living at Canonbury Square, Orwell wrote an article on "British Cookery", complete with recipes, commissioned by the British Council. Given the post-war shortages, both parties agreed not to publish it.[109] His sister Marjorie died of kidney disease in May and shortly after, on 22 May 1946, Orwell set off to live on the Isle of Jura at a house known as Barnhill.[110]

This was an abandoned farmhouse with outbuildings near the northern end of the island, situated at the end of a five-mile (8 km), heavily rutted track from Ardlussa, where the owners lived. Conditions at the farmhouse were primitive but the natural history and the challenge of improving the place appealed to Orwell. His sister Avril accompanied him there and young novelist Paul Potts made up the party. In July Susan Watson arrived with Orwell's son Richard. Tensions developed and Potts departed after one of his manuscripts was used to light the fire. Orwell meanwhile set to work on *Nineteen Eighty-Four*. Later Susan Watson's boyfriend David Holbrook arrived. A fan of Orwell since school days, he found the reality very different, with Orwell hostile and disagreeable probably because of Holbrook's membership of the Communist Party.[111] Susan Watson could no longer stand being with Avril and she and her boyfriend left.

Orwell returned to London in late 1946 and picked up his literary journalism again. Now a well-known writer, he was swamped with work. Apart from a visit to Jura in the new year he stayed in London for one of the coldest British winters on record and with such a national shortage of fuel that he burnt his furniture and his child's toys. The heavy smog in the days before the Clean Air Act 1956 did little to help his health about which he was reticent, keeping clear of medical attention. Meanwhile, he had to cope with rival claims of publishers Gollancz and Warburg for publishing rights. About this time he co-edited a collection titled *British Pamphleteers* with Reginald Reynolds. As a result of the success of *Animal Farm*, Orwell was expecting a large bill from the Inland Revenue and he contacted a firm of accountants of which the senior partner was Jack Harrison. The firm advised Orwell to establish a company to own his copyright and to receive his royalties and set up a "service agreement" so that he could draw a salary. Such a company "George Orwell Productions Ltd" (GOP Ltd) was set up on 12 September 1947 although the service agreement was not then put into effect. Jack Harrison left the details at this stage to junior colleagues.[112]

Orwell left London for Jura on 10 April 1947.[12] In July he ended the lease on the Wallington cottage.[113] Back on Jura he worked on *Nineteen Eighty-Four* and made good progress. During that time his sister's family visited, and Orwell led a disastrous boating expedition, on 19 August,[114] which nearly led to loss of life whilst trying to cross the notorious Gulf of Corryvreckan and gave him a soaking which was not good for his health. In December a chest specialist was summoned from Glasgow who pronounced Orwell seriously ill and a week before Christmas 1947 he was in Hairmyres Hospital in East Kilbride, then a small village in the countryside, on the outskirts of Glasgow. Tuberculosis was diagnosed and the request for permission to import streptomycin to treat Orwell went as far as Aneurin Bevan, then Minister of Health. David

Astor helped with supply and payment and Orwell began his course of streptomycin on 19 or 20 February 1948.[115] By the end of July 1948 Orwell was able to return to Jura and by December he had finished the manuscript of *Nineteen Eighty-Four*. In January 1949, in a very weak condition, he set off for a sanatorium at Cranham, Gloucestershire, escorted by Richard Rees.

The sanatorium at Cranham consisted of a series of small wooden chalets or huts in a remote part of the Cotswolds near Stroud. Visitors were shocked by Orwell's appearance and concerned by the shortcomings and ineffectiveness of the treatment. Friends were worried about his finances, but by now he was comparatively well-off. He was writing to many of his friends, including Jacintha Buddicom, who had "rediscovered" him, and in March 1949, was visited by Celia Kirwan. Kirwan had just started working for a Foreign Office unit, the Information Research Department, set up by the Labour government to publish anti-communist propaganda, and Orwell gave her a list of people he considered to be unsuitable as IRD authors because of their pro-communist leanings. Orwell's list, not published until 2003, consisted mainly of writers but also included actors and Labour MPs.[104][116] Orwell received more streptomycin treatment and improved slightly. In June 1949 *Nineteen Eighty-Four* was published to immediate critical and popular acclaim.

References:
1. ^ "George Orwell". UCL Orwell Archives. Archived from the original on 27 February 2009. Retrieved 7 November 2008.
2. ^ "George Orwell". *The British Library*. Retrieved 4 October 2019.

^ "Why I Write" in The Collected Essays, Journalism and Letters of George Orwell Volume 1: An Age Like This 1945–1950 p. 23. (Penguin)

^ Orwell, George (1968) [1958]. Bott, George (ed.). *Selected Writings*. London: Heinemann. p. 103. ISBN 978-0435136758. Every line of serious work that I have written since 1936 has been written, directly or indirectly, *against* totalitarianism and *for* democratic socialism, as I understand it. [italics in original]

^ Gale, Steven H. (1996). *Encyclopedia of British Humorists: Geoffrey Chaucer to John Cleese, Volume 1*. Taylor & Francis. p. 823.

^ "George Orwell | Books | The Guardian". *the Guardian*. Retrieved 4 October 2019.

^ "The 50 greatest British writers since 1945". *The Times*. 5 January 2008. Retrieved 7 January 2014.

^ Robert McCrum, *The Observer*, 10 May 2009

^ "Home : Oxford English Dictionary". *www.oed.com*. Retrieved 2 September 2017.

.^ Crick, Bernard (2004). "Eric Arthur Blair [*pseud.* George Orwell] (1903–1950)". *Oxford Dictionary of National Biography*. Oxford, England, United Kingdom: Oxford University Press.

.^ Jump up to:*a b* Stansky, Peter; Abrahams, William (1994). "From Bengal to St Cyprian's". *The unknown Orwell: Orwell, the transformation*. Stanford, California, United States: Stanford University Press. pp. 5–12. ISBN 978-0804723428.

.^ Jump up to:*a b c d e f g h i j k l m* Taylor, D.J. (2003). *Orwell: The Life*. Henry Holt and Company. ISBN 978-0805074734.

.^ Orwell, George (February 1937). "8". *The Road to Wigan Pier*. Left Book Club. p. 1.

.^ Haleem, Suhail (11 August 2014). "The Indian Animal Farm where Orwell was born". *BBC News*.

.^ Jump up to:*a b* Crick (1982), p. 48

.^ "Renovation of British Author George Orwell's house in Motihari begins". *IANS*. news.biharprabha.com. Archived from the original on 29 June 2014. Retrieved 26 June2014.

.^ A Kind of Compulsion 1903–36, xviii

.^ Bowker, Gordon. "George Orwell": 21.

.^ "Royal Eastbourne Golf Club – Hambro Bowl". Regc.unospace.net. Archived from the original on 28 April 2011. Retrieved 21 October 2010.

.^ Bowker p. 30

.^ Jacob, Alaric (1984). "Sharing Orwell's Joys, but not his Fears". In Norris, Christopher (ed.). *Inside the Myth*. Lawrence and Wishart.

.^ Jump up to:*a b c d e* Buddicom, Jacintha (1974). *Eric and Us*. Frewin. ISBN 978-0856320767.

.^ "Henley and South Oxfordshire Standard". 2 October 1914.

.^ "Henley and South Oxfordshire Standard". 21 July 1916.

25.^ Jacintha Buddicom, *Eric and Us*, p. 58

26.^ Jump up to:*a b c d e* Wadhams, Stephen (1984). "Remembering Orwell". Penguin.

27.^ Jump up to:*a b c* Connolly, Cyril (1973) [1938]. *Enemies of Promise*. London: Deutsch. ISBN 978-0233964881.

28.^ Binns, Ronald (2018). *Orwell in Southwold*. Zoilus Press. ISBN 978-1999735920.

29.^ *A Kind of Compulsion*, p. 87, gives Blair as 7th of *29* successful candidates, and 21st of the 23 successful candidates who passed the Indian Imperial Police riding test, in September 1922.

30.^ *The India Office and Burma Office List: 1927*. Harrison & Sons, Ltd. 1927. p. 514.

31.^ Jump up to:*a b* UK Retail Price Index inflation figures are based on data from Clark, Gregory (2017). "The Annual RPI and Average Earnings for Britain, 1209 to Present (New Series)". *MeasuringWorth*. Retrieved 2 February 2020.

32.^ *The Combined Civil List for India: January 1923*. The Pioneer Press. 1923. p. 399.

33.^ *The India Office and Burma Office List: 1923*. Harrison & Sons, Ltd. 1923. p. 396.

34.^ Stansky & Abrahams, *The Unknown Orwell*, pp. 170–71

35.^ Jump up to:*a b* Michael Shelden *Orwell: The Authorised Biography*, William Heinemann, 1991

36.^ *The Combined Civil List for India: July–September 1925*. The Pioneer Press. 1925. p. 409.

37.^ *A Kind of Compulsion, 1903–36*, p. 87

38.^ Emma Larkin, Introduction, *Burmese Days*, Penguin Classics edition, 2009

39.^ *The India Office and Burma Office List: 1929*. Harrison & Sons, Ltd. 1929. p. 894.

40.^ Crick (1982), p. 122

41.^ Stansky & Abrahams, *The Unknown Orwell*, p. 195

42.^ Ruth Pitter *BBC Overseas Service broadcast*, 3 January 1956

43.^ Plaque #2825 on Open Plaques.

44.^ Stansky & Abrahams, *The Unknown Orwell*, p. 204

45.^ *A Kind of Compulsion* (1903–36), p. 113

46.^ Stansky & Abrahams, *The Unknown Orwell*, p. 216

47.^ R.S. Peters (1974). *A Boy's View of George Orwell* Psychology and Ethical Development. Allen & Unwin

48.^ Stansky & Abrahams, p. 230 *The Unknown Orwell*

49.^ Jump up to:*a b* Stella Judt "I once met George Orwell" in *I once Met* 1996

50.^ "Discovery of 'drunk and incapable' arrest record shows Orwell's 'honesty'". *ucl.ac.uk*. 4 December 2014. Archived from the original on 6 January 2015. Retrieved 25 February2015.

51.^ Crick (1982), p. 221

52.^ Avril Dunn *My Brother George Orwell* Twentieth Century 1961

53.^ Voorhees (1986: 11)

^ Leys, Simon (6 May 2011). "The Intimate Orwell". *The New York Review of Books*. Retrieved 6 May 2011.

^ Orwell, Sonia and Angus, Ian (eds.)*Orwell: An Age Like This*, letters 31 and 33 New York: Harcourt, Brace & World)

^ "George Orwell: from Animal Farm to Zog, an A–Z of Orwell". The Telegraph. 20 March 2018.

^ Stansky & Abrahams, *Orwell:The Transformation* pp. 100–01

^ A Kind of Compulsion, p. 392

^ D. J. Taylor *Orwell: The Life* Chatto & Windus 2003

^ Clarke, Ben. "George Orwell, Jack Hilton, and the Working Class." *Review of English Studies* 67.281 (2016) 764–85.

^ A Kind of Compulsion, p. 457

^ A Kind of Compulsion, p. 450. The Road to Wigan Pier Diary

^ A Kind of Compulsion, p. 468

^ "Freedom of Information, National Archives" http://www.nationalarchives.gov.uk/releases/2005/highlights_july/july19/default.htm)

^ "Notes on the Spanish Militias" in Orwell in Spain, p. 278

^ Haycock, *I Am Spain* (2013), 152

^ John McNair – Interview with Ian Angus UCL 1964

^ See article by Iain King on Orwell's war experiences, here.

^ Letter to Eileen Blair April 1937 in *The Collected Essays, Journalism and Letters of George Orwell Volume 1 – An Age Like This 1945–1950* p. 296 (Penguin)

^ Jump up to:*a b* Hicks, Granville (18 May 1952). "George Orwell's Prelude in Spain". *New York Times*.

^ Bowker, p. 216

^ "The accusation of espionage against the P.O.U.M. rested solely upon articles in the Communist press and the activities of the Communist-controlled secret police." *Homage to Catalonia* p. 168. Penguin, 1980

^ Jump up to:*a b* "Newsinger, John "Orwell and the Spanish Revolution" *International Socialism Journal*Issue 62 Spring 1994". Pubs.socialistreviewindex.org.uk. Retrieved 21 October 2010.

^ Bowker, quoting Orwell in Homage To Catalonia, p. 219

^ "Harry Milton – The Man Who Saved Orwell". Hoover Institution. Archived from the original on 20 June 2015. Retrieved 23 December 2008.

^ Taylor (2003: 228–29))

^ Gordon Bowker, Orwell, p. 218 ISBN 978-0349115511

^ Facing Unpleasant Facts, p. xxix, Secker & Warburg, 2000

^ Facing Unpleasant Facts, pp. 31, 224

80.^ "Gordon Bowker: Orwell's London". theorwellprise.co.uk. Retrieved 2 February 2011.

81.^ "Another piece of the puzzle – Charles' George Orwell Links". Netcharles.com. Archived from the original on 19 June 2010. Retrieved 21 October 2010.

82.^ "George Orwell Biography". Paralumun.com. Archived from the original on 27 April 2011. Retrieved 21 October 2010.

83.^ "The Orwell Prize". Orwelldiaries.wordpress.com. 16 August 2010. Retrieved 21 October 2010.

84.^ Connelly, Mark (2018). *George Orwell: A Literary Companion*. McFarland. p. 17.

85.^ *A Patriot After All, 1940–41*, p. xvii 1998 Secker & Warburg

86.^ Churchwell, Sarah. "Diaries". *New Statesman*. Retrieved 22 October 2018.

87.^ "About George Orwell". *www.theguardian.com – Newsroom*. Retrieved 2 September2017.

88.^ *A Patriot After All*, p. xviii

89.^ Frances Stonor Saunders, *Who Paid the Piper?*, p. 160

90.^ *The Collected Essays, Journalism and Letters of George Orwell Volume 2 – My Country Right or Left 1940–1943* p. 40 (Penguin)

91.^ *A Patriot After All 1940–1941*, p. 522

92.^ Crick (1982), pp. 432–33

93.^ Gordon Bowker (2013). *George Orwell*. Little, Brown Book Group. pp. 309–10. ISBN 978-1405528054.

94.^ "Recordings Capture Writers' Voices Off The Page Listen Queue". NPR. Retrieved 5 November 2016.

95.^ Khan, Urmeen (4 June 2009). "BBC tried to take George Orwell off air because of 'unattractive' voice". *Daily Telegraph*. Retrieved 5 November 2016. The BBC tried to take the author George Orwell off air because his voice was "unattractive", according to archive documents released by the corporation...no recording of Orwell's voice survives but contemporaries—such as the artist Lucian Freud—have described it as "monotonous" with "no power".

96.^ Rodden (1989)

97.^ Crick (1982)

98.^ Jump up to:*a b* Crick, Bernard R. (1980). *George Orwell: A Life*. Boston: Little, Brown and Company. ISBN 978-0316161121.

99.^ Muggeridge, Malcolm (1962). "Burmese Days *(Introduction)*". Time Inc. Muggeridge recalls that he asked Orwell if such broadcasts were useful, "'Perhaps not', he said, somewhat crestfallen. He added, more cheerfully, that anyway, no one could pick up the broadcasts except on short-wave sets which cost about the equivalent of an Indian labourer's earnings over 10 years"

100.^ *Two Wasted Years*, 1943, p. xxi, Secker & Warburg, 2001

1.^ *I Have Tried to Tell the Truth*, p. xv. Secker & Warburg, 2001
2.^ Orwell, G.; Davison, P. (1999). *I Have Tried to Tell the Truth*. London: Secker & Warburg. ISBN 978-0436203701.
3.^ *I Have Tried to Tell the Truth*, p. xxix
4.^ Jump up to:*a b* Garton Ash, Timothy (25 September 2003). "Orwell's List". *The New York Review of Books*. Archived from the original on 5 March 2016. Retrieved 26 April 2016.
5.^ Caute, David (2009). *Politics and the Novel during the Cold War*. New Brunswick, NJ: Transaction Publishers. p. 79. ISBN 978-1412811613.
6.^ "He had led a quiet life as Richard Blair, not 'Richard Orwell'": Shelden (1991: 398; 489)
7.^ Orwell: Collected Works, I Have Tried to Tell the Truth, p. 283
8.^ "Remembering Jura, Richard Blair". Theorwellprize.co.uk. 5 October 2012. Retrieved 14 May 2014.
9.^ "The Orwell Prize | Life and Work – Exclusive Access to the Orwell Archive". Archived from the original on 10 December 2007.
0.^ "Barnhill". is located at 56°06′39″N 5°41′30″W (British national grid reference systemNR705970)
1.^ David Holbrook in Stephen Wadham's *Remembering Orwell* Penguin Books 1984
2.^ Jump up to:*a b c d e* "Tim Carroll 'A writer wronged'". *The Sunday Times*. Timesonline.co.uk. 15 August 2014. Retrieved 14 May 2014.
3.^ Crick (1982), p. 530
4.^ Orwell: Collected Works, *It Is What I Think*, p. xx, *Daily Telegraph*, 2 December 2013, [1]
5.^ It Is what I Think, p. 274
6.^ Ezard, John (21 June 2003). "Blair's babe: Did love turn Orwell into a government stooge?". *The Guardian*. London.